Gallimaufry & Farrago

poems by

Kathleen Balma

Finishing Line Press
Georgetown, Kentucky

Gallimaufry & Farrago

Copyright © 2018 by Kathleen Balma
ISBN 978-1-63534-612-1 First Edition
All rights reserved under International and Pan-American Copyright Conventions. No part of this book may be reproduced in any manner whatsoever without written permission from the publisher, except in the case of brief quotations embodied in critical articles and reviews.

ACKNOWLEDGMENTS

Many thanks to the proprietors of Rivendell Writers' Colony for providing time, space, and monetary support for the completion of this chapbook, and to the editors of the following publications in which these poems first appeared, sometimes in earlier versions:

Atlanta Review, The Café Review, Calliope, Cardinal Points, Chiron Review, Contemporary Verse 2, Crab Orchard Review, Crate, Cutbank, decomP, Drunken Boat, Dunes Review, Fugue, The Hopkins Review, Hotel Amerika, The Journal, New Haven Review, PMS: poemmemoirstory, Prelude, Prick of the Spindle, Puerto del Sol, Rattle, Salamander, Sixth Finch, storySouth, and *Sugar House Review.*

"Dotage" appears in the *Montreal International Poetry Prize Global Poetry Anthology 2015.* "The Fountain of Relative Age" was reprinted in *The Maple Leaf Rag VI: An Anthology of Poetic Writings from New Orleans.* "From Your Hostess at the T & A Museum" appears in *Pushcart Prize XXXVII.* "Poem Poem Poem Poem Poem" was republished by the American Tinnitus Association.

Publisher: Leah Maines
Editor: Christen Kincaid
Cover Art: Megan Whitmarsh
Author Photo: Niels Behrman
Cover Design: Elizabeth Maines McCleavy

Printed in the USA on acid-free paper.
Order online: www.finishinglinepress.com
          also available on amazon.com

Author inquiries and mail orders:
Finishing Line Press
P. O. Box 1626
Georgetown, Kentucky 40324
U. S. A.

Table of Contents

For Oyster Shuckers 1
Abraham, Honestly 2
The Fountain of Relative Age 4
Somewhere a Town 5
Revelation at the Invisible Gun Show 6
Black Hole Horizon 7
The Forgiveness Project 8
Poem on the Verge of a Nervous Breakdown 9
Summer Camp for Sirens 10
A Tour of Pompeii's Red-Light District 11
Stopping Time Is not as Useful as We Thought 13
Elegy for Florence 14
What the Traveler Knows 15
Genetically Modified Crop Conspiracies 16
Dramatic Dichotologue 17
Dotage 18
From Your Hostess at the T & A Museum 19
The Causes of Cyclone Formation Aren't Well
    Understood 20
Escape from the Abhorrent Vacuum 22
Poem Poem Poem Poem Poem 23
Spaghetti Midwestern 24
What Do Ghosts Need? 25
Highlights from an Interview with the Author 27
Singularity 30
Temporary Empathy 32
Lunch Alone at Antoine's, September 2015 33

For Oyster Shuckers

The man prying open my meal
has a book. Took him 25 years
to write. About his life,
which he was living
while penning. That's why it
took so long. That, and of course,
the oysters. (Had to let his first
wife go; he *wanted*
to leave New York, take her
home. She said, No.)
His tip jar's not on empty,
but close. Oh baby,
I don't want to lose you.
I'm on the half shell.

Abraham, Honestly

> "With his own two hands, Abe Lincoln built the log cabin he was born in."
> —from an American college student's history paper

Theory 1: Out-of-Body Abe

The ghostly glob of fetal Abraham sneaks out of his mother's womb at night with architecture on his budding mind. In the first few months the Lincoln bean can barely hold a toothpick, let alone a log, so he darts around his neighbor's place, plotting floor plans and examining crannies. By month two his heart's really in it. By mid-trimester he's using his tail to smooth out the mud mortar of his neighbor's house. **Mudd**, he thinks, and feels his very first shiver. By month five he's chopping thick stripes of wood by the light of his prenatal halo. By month six he's strapping logs to his unborn back and floating them across miles of Kentucky airspace. By month seven he's all over the roof like a Christmas specter. By month eight his newly lit neurons are sparkling up the lawn as he flaps back and forth from womb to hearth, nesting like there's no state like home, no place like tomorrow.

Theory 2: Born-Again Abe

When you make a house of your heart, no assembly is required, but some laying on of hands may be.

Theory 3: Authorial Abe

Like many Abrahams before him, Lincoln enjoys limited omniscience whenever he writes speeches, treaties, bills, or commandments, and this has begun to affect his mind in arboreal ways. He often imagines what it must have been like for his Pa to construct their homestead. How many times had the teenage Lincoln built that same boxy lodge in his mind, amputating trees and sanding them to naked plainness, putting, perhaps, more care into it than his own father had? This daydream kicks in like a nervous tick when he loses things, and for every log he stacks on his imaginary abode, a windy sigh rushes through the grassy blades of his beard. Since the war began, he's been adding rooms that were never there in his youth, and the walls are getting higher, so high the house is now a tower he must climb and climb.

The Fountain of Relative Age

You dip in, become who you are.

A fun-loving fitness coach finally resembles
the twelve-year-old boy he emits.
His cannonballs punctuate bold *yippees*.

A third grade belle in terrycloth wrap, flush
with spelling bee medals, emerges a ripe twenty-two.
The neighborhood sociopath truncates
to toddler. He steps out of his blue
uniform and wails, confused. Responsibilities,

rights and roles reassigned
according to each new body, the world adjusts!

Except for those who don't change, who swim for hours
unaffected. These get out, dry off, scarf down
their tuna salad sandwich halves, their Gala apple slices,
wondering why everyone took off.

Somewhere a Town

Somewhere a town celebrates by having a giant tomato fight. They bring the tomatoes in trucks and can't wait to pummel and be pummeled. After the pummeling, they slosh down juicy streets and pose as swimmers in shallow rivers of pulp while sopping journalists snap their pictures. Somewhere else a town celebrates by running away from bulls, or by watching others run away from bulls. Somewhere else a town celebrates by racing horses around sharp-cornered streets at maximum speed. Each horse is named for a different animal, each fauna for a hoary neighborhood. One horse is a giraffe. (I know because I have a friend from the giraffe neighborhood.) One horse may also be a bull. That horse may be under the impression that he is supposed to be in another town, chasing people. Somewhere else a town celebrates by having an orange fight. This is a more solid than liquid celebration, due to the peels. Liquid celebrations do not often involve large amounts of tomatoes, bulls, horses, giraffes, oranges, or decorum, and thank goodness for that, or we might all be wandering around half limpid, wondering how to throw fruit and run from animals in a polite and professional manner. Somewhere a town of bulls celebrates by springing leaks in people.

Revelation at the Invisible Gun Show

A dapper man stands
behind empty display,

baby powder in hand.
He sprinkles the talcum;

a weapon appears to appear.
It's not like any we've ever

never seen. First sight:
the almost outline of barrel

and grip beneath drops of white.
The salesman touches the solid

nada, spreads the dust
just so, and all the gun parts start

to show (now muzzle, now clip)
—a nude, small caliber soul.

How to know if rounds
are in those spirit chambers,

haunting? All the bullets
for this unobserved piece,

to eyes untrained
in unseen things

are loud in sound
if not in hue, and piercing.

Black Hole Horizon

I'm in flux with a TV alien, the best sad thing that's happened to me all year. He's in flux with someone else, of course. They live in different macrocosms. My chances with him aren't great either, I know, but the odds of my nonfictional self bumping into his fictional one are actually much better than the odds of two universes overlapping and forming a handy little doorway, so I'm in a much better position than the long lost girlfriend. She'll keep pining away in her parallel world, wishing she had the weekly window into his life that millions enjoy, or at least an identical night sky. I'll keep polishing the glass of my flat-screen crystal ball and writing her farther and farther into the back of his mind. Until he can barely remember what her face looks like. Until she's just another dot on his bright and busy page.

The Forgiveness Project

—after Szymborska

Under what conditions should one admit wrongdoing?
Is confessing in a dream as good as in a booth?
Who goes first?
Are there age restrictions?
Do the dead get a shot?

Who runs the project and for how long?
Are reservations and appointments a must,
or is it first come, first served?
Is there a suggestion box? A gift registry?
Will I need a witness?

When the apology part is over,
should all spilled secrets be tagged and catalogued?
Accidents, sins, mistakes, peccadilloes …
who decides what's what?
Do records remain sealed?

Do poems count as admissions of guilt? Do paintings?
Are confessional poems by victims
filed under A for *Allegations*
during pax audits and quarrel inventories?
Is the Forgiveness Librarian discrete? Is she happy?

After the project, will a pardon be a privilege,
a rite of passage, or both? Is there a prize for best entry?
Do animals participate? Do plants?
Will a new holiday mark the end of resentment?
Are "I Forgave Today" stickers at the exit?

Poem on the Verge of a Nervous Breakdown

—for Almodóvar

In my favorite movie a woman lights a fire in her bed
after trying all day to find her married lover,
to tell him she is pregnant. Now I know
what you're thinking: the fire is a metaphor
for passion, but that's not really what I mean.
What I mean is I like the idea of a fire
—a *real* fire—being lit in someone's bed
who has been trying all day to find her married lover
and tell him she is pregnant, but instead
keeps finding her lover's wife, and ends up
with no lover, no bed, and no abortion.

This blazing bed comes to her
at a time in her life when a blazing bed
is the least absurd thing that could happen,
so she does what anyone would do.
She stands there coughing like an idiot,
then goes back to the kitchen.
I like to imagine in that moment of standing
that she is thinking about her bed,
wondering if it's ever been quite that hot before
and if so, when? I imagine she looks
at her sunny fire and sees herself

reflected there, as in an orange mirror,
then remembers all her really good sex
happened somewhere else. *The roof!*
she thinks, and turns for the door
just in time for the Spanish fire brigade
to burst in like flames and discover her.

Summer Camp for Sirens

Here we learn to deep-freeze Dreamsicles, lift bunks at wrong angles until our spines kneel down inside our backs, and handwrite Thank You cards with one athletic, cursive hand while waving with the limp-wristed other. Our camp uniforms are coveralls covered in flags. We get a new flag for everything we learn. We even get a new flag for learning how to earn a new flag! Holidays we don dress uniforms (called *dressforms*) with dress flags (called *drags*). Then they teach us the language of eyes, how to ask for help, how to feign. We are taught never to talk of this. Our organs do our talking for us. The mouth of all pain is called the brain. This is where the miracle of early rising happens, and where the shopping cart turns in-law to the artificial heart. Because cars are still the best leg technology we have, the evening staff teach us to wheel-walk on land. The last day they take us to a lake, where we blare and hum at kayaks, milky bottles all around. Then they take us straight back to camp, let us cry it out.

A Tour of Pompeii's Red-Light District

A stone bed complete
with stone pillow

in an office the size
of an outhouse.

Along the top
edge of hall

(where a wall-
paper border

might go) is porn so old
we feel safe

saying "art"
and smiling.

Some men took time
to etch their praise

or customer
service complaint:

Flora gives good head!
Octavia has the clap!

No poems here,
it seems—

this blunt graffiti
all that's left.

No bodies either, now,
just ghastly casts

in vast museums, or
for those who hear

through time and ash:
ghostly gasps.

Stopping Time Is Not as Useful as We Thought

At first we simply wander, delighted with frozen smoke curls and uplifted forks in our favorite diner; the remarkable faces of drivers mid-crash; the way pellets of rain disappear where we walk, leaving body-shaped paths in the air. We consider travel, but the roads are littered with stilled cars and neither of us flies. Even looting isn't as easy as we supposed: the thyme green sofa we ogle is burdensome to carry, so we choose a hearthrug with beige mountain shapes that reminds us of *Brigadoon* and the seventies. We balance the shag on our shoulders and drag two bags full of gallimaufry and farrago from that vintage garb shop down the road. The only other things we really need now are your extra-wide dress shoes, which will have to be mail-ordered post pause, and a house, which still feels remote and chimerical, like Dalí. Even good deeds are unexpectedly complex, though we eventually choose to pickpocket the fob of a petrified doctor in white coat and vest, then slip script pads in the clutch bag of a bedfast hatmaker while she freeze-weeps on an Irish "magic hanky." (Now it's a hanky. Now it's a bonnet. Now it's a hanky again.)

Elegy for Florence

Before the horrid caving in of Brunelleschi's Duomo
and the subsequent plunk of that romantic perch
Ponte Vecchio—the Florentines' only
pre-World War bridge—its jewelry stores
dropping gold in the river Arno,
secret passageways spilling out tour guides and rats;
before the great Uffizi museum collapsed
to a dune of rocks and Botticelli rags
(They now sell these for a pittance in Pisa.);
before the David had been reduced
to a cracked and glued affair
in the Louvre basement; before Via Ricasoli was more rubble
than flare, and flames had destroyed San Lorenzo;
before you and I knew a word like "divorce,"
you were my *paese*, your city my home.

What the Traveler Knows

Every country is a cure for something;
every cobblestone a lozenge
for some scratchy, sore spot
in your pedestrian head; every skyline
a pointy heavenscape of exclamation marks,
cheering you on. If you are irksome and rude
in your own land, there is another
where you are witty and direct; your voice,
once a pastel whine, now an atonal woodwind
of desire. If you are hideous
in your hometown, there is a locale
where you can melt the locals
with your sunless eyes
and hold your wire-haired head high while
an effervescent flow of admirers
bubbles from the sacred streets,
winking and circling you on bikes.
You have only to find it, your stopping place,
find it and let it remake you from the *terra* up.
Why make amends when you can make haste?
Look there, that palace, this tower,
yonder mountain peak—it's the view
you were born to see, the perfect
finish to the shelf song of your life
so far. The end. Keep looking.
The end. Maybe tomorrow. The end.
Almost there. The end.

Genetically Modified Crop Conspiracies

1.

Your corn farm is a field of spies. Its ears are eavesdropping, each root a cochlear maize device implanted in high tech soil to listen in. Crop circles are circling the station wagons, buttering themselves for battle. Your grits will not save you. Your good guys with grits will not save you. Who will save you? Who will save you from the Frankenstalks? Your hungry, of course. Your tractors. Your cows and horses, longing to eat grain. Feed them these: your homegrown corn dogs of war, your frenemies on the cob. Feed them, and know peas and hominy.

2.

Smart soybeans are in league with Mexicans. They want to take over the Heartland. Soy: I am (not the impermanent "I am fine" but the permanent "I am from here"). Vegetarians aid the Soy-Mexican team, their larders full of tofu. «*Soy de aquí.*»   Say it fast and it rhymes with soybean.

3.

Pigs will soon be crossbred with vedge, their swine bulbs buried like mandrakes. (How delicious is the porkiflower! How rich are oinccoli and hamfalfa sprouts!) No, no plantimals were harmed for this salad. Picked but never pulled out by the hooves, they live to sprout again. But *think*, will you? Who might use them for food and who for torture? *This little piggy went to black ops. This little piggy flew drones. This little piggy got five stars. This little piggy got cloned. This little piggy cried, "Dress me! Dress me! Dress me!" all the way home.*

Dramatic Dichotologue

It's good to be bilingual. Almost makes up
for the other bi thing about me. Not quite family, but step-

whatsit, or great doohickey twice removed
on your ex-fairy-godmother's side. Still, I'm something

like your Aunt David, and if the Queen ever dies
I'm in the line of succession. Truthfully, I prefer

circles to lines. "Circle of succession"
has a nice ring. Like Knights of the Round Table

only sexier. You may think it's hard to be sexier
than a circumference of metal-clad men, but I swear by

all the bivalves in an errant chef's paella
that my circuit is more heartthrob than King Arthur's.

So would Casanova. He'd swear on a stack of pizzas,
florins, and halos, 'cause that's how Giacomo rolls.

I can't help but epicene. Head doctors named me.
They were torn between bi- and pan-, but Pan complained.

Turns out he's not a fan, either. He'll shag
any cloven beast but me. His loss.

I've never loved by halves. The army was
pleased in Top Secret—something about my

expertise at double time and scientists always inviting me
to experiments. Yes, the bars are full of lab jockeys,

but why complain? I haven't had this much
airtime since David Bowie died and brought me

four chambers closer to the throne.

Dotage

Lover, let's age swap: you lunge backwards and slough off
a double decker of years. I'll slide into a sadder sack of myself

in time-lapse photography and wait. It wouldn't take
long for you not to show up. The reverse of us

doesn't work. The plus and minus of perv: *man's* perk. Could you then,
as you are nonce, touch the future me as I will want (reverb)

to be (re)touched? Pen stripling comfort to my sag and stitch,
some message in a rocket for a youer me to read?

I would like to benefit from that missive tout suite, but who am I
to peep on my elder ego? She might slap me, or worse:

pity. Or—twist in plot—she may surprise us both and not
want touch at all. She may be busy with more anile tastes,

quilting and such, collecting obliques. She may take up frottage
with a known cuckold. (Mattress ticking's the rub: better plain,

unsoiled.) A more selfishly sufficient bag may never live,
unquaked by anything but the cackle arts.

Yet, she'll be a *product* of caress. My someday skin
must bear that. So, on the svelte chance you might

want her, lover, I'd send you off to that there now
at my nower self's expense.

From Your Hostess at the T & A Museum

If you will not tip me for my dance, tip me for daring to ask. Or if, having stared at me directly for the duration of a song or two, you still did not manage to see me, as you claim, then tip me for what you see now: the perfect circumference of twin areolae, one torso a la Aphrodite statue, one triangle of cloth bundling *L'Origine du monde* and pointing like an arrow to the masculine earth. Do you doubt that the artist tipped *his* model? Oh, but you're right: there is that old understanding between painters and nudes. Tit for dab, so to speak. Similarly, artists and restaurateurs have sometimes exchanged a mouthful for an eye feast (dab for tidbit, slapdash for tiddlywink). Tip me, then, in calories; offer me a slice of lime split wide over the edge of a beverage. Tip me for staring back so hard it puts even *Olympia* to shame and makes her *chat noire* slink ever closer to her overlooked and under-rendered black maid. Tip me, at least, for carrying so many geometrician's tools: the circle, the triangle, the rectangular bills tucked beneath such finite and measurable bikini lines. Tip me for my burlesque, crescent-shaped ass. Tip me for what you don't see: the abstract; the invisible; the squiggly outline of a model's brain matter in silhouette; negative space plastered between fleshy objects like some happy vacuum, giving form to the nothingness between us.

The Causes of Cyclone Formation Aren't Well Understood

1

Yes, it's true: stunted rubes are our only fruits. They follow the yellow bric-a-brac of cornfield and orchard, look to wind vanes for brain-heart direction, then tomcat home in sundry shades of redneck.

2

The breeze here gets so sick of us, it spits out true green cumuli, then sets that funnel cake cloud down and spins it like a Tilt-a-Whirl all over our broke town, sprouting yard sales where none have been.

3

An oak fought bravely, but died defending its plot. Surviving it are one small girl child, dog, and aunt.

4

What I remember seeing: the twirling gale ate the middles of things, left neat rows of rooftops for blocks and blocks. (Somewhere in all this mess is my baton.)

5

To the cellar! No cellar? Down a basement! No basement? Under stairs! No stairs? In a bathtub! No tub? Find a ditch! No ditch? Tag: you're a witch!

6

Wizard of Oz works as a film because so few see midlands as anything but a place for flight, and even a winged grudge monkey has more social cachet than a farmer.

7

A weatherman is an elemental wiz. As such, he can do nothing but try to predict what air already knows, then instruct you to use the dead's shoes to find a way home.

Escape from the Abhorrent Vacuum

What if nature is tired of being a mother,
of gendered metaphors splayed

in her honor, the suckling pigs of poetry,
obscene apple muzzles shoved snugly

under their snouts? What if she is ten kinds of trans:
transitory, transmigrant, a transplanted liver

filtering the good word from the gaff … ? What if she isn't
a she at all, but a beautiful bearded mountain

man, all oceanic swagger and volcanic lisp?
No remedy for identity. No one-off spring

for the inner-wintered, homoseasonal
depressed. Diagnosis: mother-obsessed.

Let's give nature a choice for once. Let him let down
his habit-bound hair, spit, grope, and swear.

Let him eat steak *and* cake. Be multi-sex
beast. Be worm. Be queen and worshipful worker

in one. A beeline made to fit. Wear it, mother. Put it on,
if only to shrug it back off, again and again and again.

Poem Poem Poem Poem Poem

There are certain white noisy things that scientists believe. When aliens contact earth they will do it by making a tonal racket from on high. They will do this celestial honking at regular intervals. They will use the honk method because space can be a raucous place and science needs replication in order to work. Recurrence must blare for belief to occur.

This alien din will most likely bloom in B flat. Various branches and twigs of study now corroborate the news that B flat has juju properties. Crocodiles are tamed by it, anomalous echoes echo it, and black holes are constantly humming it. Add to this the true events in my cousin's ears, and the reduplication of B flat magic is overwhelming. Ear anecdote:

My cousin the jazz percussionist woke one day to the opposite of deafness. His eardrums had acquired a heightened tuning in to even the smallest sounds. Tapping fingers on a table; dog nails clicking on stairs; the clink of fork against knife, plate, or tooth—auditorture. Add to hyperacusis a high-pitched ring in B flat. This ringing never went away. Not leaving is a kind of repetition. Drum roll for conclusions, please:

If my cousin ever hears the alien note, it could kill him, tame him, cure him, convert him, make him spill something hot, or drive him insane. Alternately, it could blend with the tinnitus within and go undetected. Doubly alternately, it could *be* the tinnitus. The aliens could be blaring their high-tech claxon right now, his super sensitive canals the only instruments picking it up. My cousin's ears may even have been specially selected to eavesdrop on this cosmic megatoot, which suggests that aliens have been in his apartment, which further suggests their Big Beep Machine (a.k.a., The Universe Horn) is already obsolete, unless they're using him as an instrumental test subject while speed-caroling more cacophonic worlds.

In order for us to trust any of this it must be repeated several times. Read this poem over and over until you believe.

Spaghetti Midwestern

If the cowboy rides the film's horizon line
past the Colorado Rockies and Topeka,

he will meet the farm hand on the other side
of the Kansas montage, and plant himself askance

in a two-bit store aisle, with rows of wide brim hats
they both admire. If they trade shirt pocket jerky,

beef for venison, then play billiards in a room
with swinging doors, the pool halls of St. Louis

will be saloons in spirit, and the strip joints of
Shy Town—for one night only—true bordellos.

Wild horses from Montana will enter at
a canter. Blink: now they're mild cows in Amish

Kentuckiana. The strip pit swimming hole
is a coal country oasis on dog days. Those outlaw

bathers? Humanesque outcroppings: limestone
cowboys for a cinematic hour. John Wayne

rides on John Deere through cornfields. His quick
draws (*presto!*) softball lobs (*adagio*). The lampoon

of Tonto fades near Cahokia. He has no mound. He is
the dead the dead don't know. The bullies of high

noon take lunch break. Gunslingers sling burgers
on the range. Painted desert: paintball forest.

What Do Ghosts Need?

A ghost needs an audience or it is pointless.
But does a ghost need a point? No.
Never mind then.

Closure, clearly, is a ghostly need.
A ghost needs a therapist.
Yes, but not a couch, for they rest floating.

A ghost needs a locus
to which it can be tethered
by an airy umbilical, but who

or what is at the other end, refusing
the quick snip? A ghost must need
an otherworldly obstetrician

or midwife. Is the psychic medium
a spirit's shrink or accoucheuse?
Neither, she's the doula.

The ghost needs a doula? Alrighty then.
Better a ghoul's doula than a hallow's evil
wet nurse. That's poltergeist stuff.

Some ghosts seem to need chains.
Some people also seem to need them.
Ghosts were once people; this makes sense.

The chain might replace the tether
in some cases, depending on whether
the role of haint is self-imposed.

To cast yourself in a shade monologue
and saturate a place with your own inner suds
is a far banshee cry from being sentenced

to limp around in a heap of invisible bling
a la Sid Vicious, neck padlocked, keyless. Sid Vicious
is definitely a ghost. He was a ghost when alive,

and a very bad one. He had no talent for it.
He was all circumstance and no pomp,
but he pulled it off. Probably lesser ghosts

hated him. Ghosts are player haters.
They need to step back, be less aura, more
trace. A ghost needs Ghandi, Twelve Steps,

or a massage of the gossamer pressure point
that leads from the power left foot
to the I-don't-give-a-damn center of the brain.

Ghost brains all have reverse Alzheimer's.
They can't forget, can't feign, can't faint
at the sight of real or ethereal blood can't pass

out can't nap through the boring bits can't
shake it off can't make light can't take
a joke can only emote, emote, emote! My God,

you ghosts, get a grip! What you need and can't get
is Mick Jagger singing "Satisfaction"
until you bleed blue luminescence from the sheer

grist of it. What you need is validation,
dear ghosts. What you need is a celestial telegram
from your mama. STOP. A ghost needs, *is*,

an S.O.S. A ghost needs Morse code
but goes with the Bat Signal.
A ghost in binary code needs one zero.

Highlights of an Interview with the Author

The Author on the Tragic Bisexual:

> Once I realized that my hand was leaning against a breast, and the breast was not moving away. Then I realized it was my own breast and felt sad.

The Author on Navy Jargon and Standing Watch:

> The midnight shift is called *balls to two* because of how it's recorded in logs: 00:00-02:00. It is thus said that midnight is a row of testicles. It is said because of how it is written. It is written: *testicles colon testicles.*

The Author on Homophonic Questionnaires:

> "Question Air"—a slogan for the anti-gravity set, or a clique of paranoid swimmers?

The Author on Gelatin, Breasts, and Implants:

> Bones with no rules, feed with no bones, boob less jelly.

The Author on Her Back Pain:

> A certain vertebrae pines for the blade of a shoulder. (The Juliet shoulder I call it, for being such a weak balcony.)

The Author on the Moon Landing:

> Houston, it's like Earth only earthier.

The Author on Seasonal Holidays:

> I celebrated winter by snogging ye olde snowmen, after which they couldn't stop mouthing, *Oh!*

The Author on the Tiny House Movement:

> Alice ate the wrong teacake and wore her home to bed.

The Author on Werewolves:

> The hairy man's revenge, world's only satellite assassin, a real dog with no real pony, a tooth parade in reverse drag.

The Author on Dating a Werewolf:

> Your ass is his only moonshine.

The Author on Plausibility and Memoir:

> There are moments from my life which don't appear to mix but are linked in the same memory strand: cleaning gun mounts the size of condos, dyeing warp threads on a loom, the

moonwalk (as in MJ, not Armstrong), happy endings (as in massage, not princess).

The Author on Emergency Room Etiquette:

You are the greater victim here.
No, you are.

The Author on Objectivity and Objectification:

I prefer to be based on observable facts, such as lights, such as cameras, such as actions.

Singularity

Job was a good man, not a wise one.
So says Maimonides, Spanish Jew and philosopher.
Job was a pussy. So say the marines. *Hoo*-ah.
Job was a covert narcissist
who saw his first wife and children
as interchangeable with the new set,
and really only wanted to be admired. So says pop
psychology. Job was a loyal subject.
So says God, an overt narcissist.
Like father, like son. Or should we say, the apple
doesn't fall far. Har har. Job was so
accustomed to a life of privilege
that when the biblical shit hit the satanic fan,
he asked, "Why me?" instead of questioning
his luck when times were easy. Job was a long-sufferer,
but not for life. So said every one of his slaves.
Job was a bit of a drama queen. So says a Greek chorus
of drag queens, who would know. Sashay.
Job was lucky to be a son of Jehovah
instead of a daughter of Troy. So say
Cassandra and Briseis. Job was a snooze fest.
So say my students. Job was a cooperative learner
who did wonderfully in math and music this year
(Numbers, Psalms), but didn't reach his potential
in science, and is too often on Cloud Nine. So said
his third grade teacher. Job was a farmer,
outstanding in his field. So said Job's obituary.
Job was neither good nor evil, but a complex amalgam
of positive and negative personality traits
that emerged or not, depending on circumstances.
So say the social sciences. Job was his DNA.
Even his mullet was predetermined.
So say the Minnesota twin studies.
Job was a good provider, but not a good lover,
and he never took me to Paris, though I begged.
So said both of his wives. Job was never

an eye for an eye kind of guy.
So say the theologians. Job was better than
his author—better, too, than this one. So say I.

Temporary Empathy

The adult human, not yet 36,
feels a spouse's hurt as keenly

as the spouse. In a few years
/ months / weeks

the couple's painshare stops.
No matter what, an alarm

goes off and one bolts up
dressed in panic.

For now they wear
a common constitution:

one nature, united.
United Nations: (deadbeat

dad at Christmas, sending
the one check per year) model

of ephemeral pity. A mammal
post-heat: sympathetic.

In heat: *stay inside or be taken.*
Only after tipping the salt

does the child see itself
in the writhing slug. The gerbil mother

sans stress feeds her young.
In medium stress she eats them.

Lunch Alone at Antoine's, September 2015

Eating an oyster here is exactly like eating an angel's
testicle. A meaty bubble pops in your mouth. Garlic butter
bursts forth. (They're all Italian,
those angels. And treacherous. They never liked
people, never understood God's perverse need
to love us best. How could he,
when he had them?) Here's proof
of my inferiority: Pink Lemonade
cocktails for twenty-five cents? Limit of three?
I'll take three. I'll also have
the special. Oysters
to start. (You *know* why.) Then Créole Shrimp
and Grits. Last: Lemon Delight.
Coffee? Yes, please. Regular. Sugar. Cream.

Kathleen Balma is the least likely person to have ever been a Fulbright Fellow. Nevertheless, she is one. She holds an MFA in Creative Writing and a Master of Library Science from Indiana University and a teaching certificate from Cambridge. Her writing awards include a Pushcart Prize and a Writer-in-Resident Fellowship from Rivendell Writers' Colony. She lives in New Orleans.

www.ingramcontent.com/pod-product-compliance
Lightning Source LLC
LaVergne TN
LVHW041601070426
835507LV00011B/1225